Fragmented:
The Demise of Unionized Construction

Glenn G. De Soto

Books are available for business or quantity discounts,
telephone the author at 951-927-0108 or e-mail at
info@crservicesinc.com

With thanks to Allen B. Bostrom, *CPA, in the Black,*
Copyright 2005, ISNB 0-9764702-0-9

Why is it that labor unions do not control the labor force in the majority of the construction market?
It's because of one simple word: fragmented.

Glenn G. De Soto explains the focal reason why unionized construction is not the favored method of construction from the owner's fragmented perspective. Glenn will also explain why construction unions need to become business (human resource) minded in today's fragmented construction environment in order to gain market-share, and he will explain what true market-share is for a construction union. In his book Glenn explains why it takes signatory union employers for a construction union to have success, he walks you through the difficulties of being a contractor in a fragmented environment, and gives you a business model and plan for success in a fragmented industry and then how to create a paradigm shift for the unionized construction sector to attract new contractors to the union methodology and thereby grow the union sector back into prominence in this construction industry.

Acknowledgments

I must thank the following individuals and organizations who have, through their influence and guidance, made me a better human being, craftsman, manager, businessman, and leader. Fred Sizelove, my high school mathematics teacher, for teaching me the value of partnering and team work; my employer, William (Bill) B. Walton, Jr., along with my staff at W.B. Walton Electric, Inc.: Jessica Lauzon, Steve Kadella, and Eric Engberson, and all the field personnel for their hard work and dedication; The International Brotherhood of Electrical Workers; The National Electrical Contractors Association; the following mentors and associates: Lee St. Pierre, David Teeter, Robert Haugen, Steve Nelson, Carl Weidimeyer, Dave Swantz, James (Jim) Berkey , Douglas (Doug) Saunders, David Lawhorn, Howard Autrey, Douglas (Doug) Chappell, William (Bill) Perez, Robert (Bob) Frost, John Brown, David Tilmont, Cecil Wynn, Robert (Bob) Goad, Richard Purper, Cliff Thompson, Craig Skomski, Sergio Pinion, Jim Smith, Pete Smith, Randy Durham, Guy Erskine, Cole Warner, Richard (Dick) Warner, Stephen (Steve) Brown, David Shankel, Rodney (Rod) Anderson, Jay Sutherland, James (Jim) Fehlman, Thomas (Tom) Ispas, Ron Schoonard, Robert (Bob) Hayes, and Elmer Kent.

I must make a special mention of Robert (Bob) Bagelnorth, who showed me the value of continual education, looking beyond myself, and giving back to the industry; and to the following individuals, who gave me great opportunities: Gerick White, Ed Johansen, Craig Clark, Richard Yeadon,

Lynn Martin, Craig Bixman, Jack Gebelin, and indirectly Laurence (Larry) Smead. I will never be able to thank them enough:

Most importantly to my mother and father, who taught me good values, and hard work, to get back up when you have been knocked down, to not just follow the crowd, to look at both sides of an issue, and to always try and be fair in my dealings. I must thank them also for the support and encouragement they always showed me in any worthy endeavor I pursued. Also to my sisters: Penny, Kerry, Angela, Lenore, and Patty, and to my brothers Philip and Kirk, for helping to shape me. To my wife, Cindy, for putting up with me, and always supporting me and prodding me; to my children, Clint, September, Grace, and Joseph, who make life amusing, difficult at times, but always entertaining; and last, but not least, to my Aunt Dorothy who keeps me grounded in my family roots and where we come from.

Table of Contents

I. Introduction

Why is it that labor unions do not control the labor force in the majority of the construction market? It's because of one simple word: fragmented. It's really that straightforward.

The construction industry at large is in a fragmented state of affairs. The only way to ever regain true majority market-share back is to approach our organizing efforts with this truth and reality in mind. This book will take you through facts, realities, and observations; then will give you a road map on how to succeed in a fragmented industry.

Let me tell you a little about myself. I was born and bred into the construction industry. My father was a contractor. As far back as I can remember, my father would take me, as a small boy, with him on weekends to clean and sweep up his shop. Quite often I would go to the job sites with him and watch construction projects. As a child, I was amazed at the way a project came together; how conflicts were always reasoned and adjusted so as to complete the project. I also marveled how the project objective was to satisfy the customer who was paying the contractor to perform to the plans and the specifications that were usually provided by the owner.

My father loved to work on remodels, which I could not understand as a child. I would think to myself, "Why would you want to waste your time and energy on projects in which you cannot see all the potential problems until after you commit and open up the walls. You could be doing new construction and having less risk and fewer headaches?" (To

1

tell the truth, I still feel that way from a risk-management way of thinking.) But what I did not realize then, that I now understand, was that my father, in his heart, was a problem solver, and loved the challenge that a remodel gave him.

What my father taught me, without using words, was to always be looking for a solution. As he looked a remodel job over, I could see his mind turning as to how he was going to solve the problem or situation that the project would give him. I noticed how he would always focus on the solution, and never get bogged down by the problems he encountered. What I learned from my father was to be a good observer, and to walk into all situations with a solution in mind; to always focus on the solution, rather than focusing on the problem. I also learned that, as a construction craft-worker, you are there to be a solution provider for the owner/employer.

And so I say to you construction union leaders, we have been focusing far too long on problems and perceived problems, and not enough on solutions. The truth is that solutions are sometimes costly and inconvenient. Solutions may also require sacrifice, and possibly a paradigm shift, that frankly most union business managers do not want to deal with. It takes hard work, political maneuvering, and dedication to change.

We, the human race, much like nature, prefer the path of least resistance, and I can tell you first-hand from my profession, Inside Wireman "Electrician", that I have seen, and experienced how energy likes to go to ground and follow the path of least resistance. The path of least resistance with our union membership is one of the many reasons that we, as a unionized sector, have been losing market share; this is because of our unwillingness to change due to inconvenience.

In my career, I have had the good fortune to be, at one time or another, at nearly every level in this construction industry. I have been an apprentice, a journeyman, a foreman, a general foreman, a superintendent, a project manager, an estimator, a design detailer, a vice president, and a CEO. This has given me insights and understandings that most in our industry, in their respective lifetime, never obtain or understand.

I have been on both sides, union and management, of the negotiating table. I have worked as a salt on non-union jobsites. I have testified before the NLRB (National Labor Relations Board) in ULPs (Unfair Labor Practices), and I have received back pay for having my rights to organize a union violated. I have been on the picket line when the occasion was needed. I have served on industry trusts and committees, and still do. I have volunteered countless hours for the industry that provides for my ability to make a living, and continually do so. I have disagreed with my leadership, union or management, when I felt they were out of line in not representing what would benefit the industry. My core belief is you must make the industry healthy first, then yourself. Once you have a healthy industry, all those in it will profit from it. With an unhealthy industry, which is the case of our current fragmented environment, only a few profit, usually at the expense of others, and society as a whole.

Now, this book may offend some union members and leaders, but is not intended to. It is intended to look at the real reason, the fragmentation of the industry, that has hampered the union movement in the construction industry. And it will show how unions can thrive in this environment -- if they are but willing to change their paradigm and way of thinking about and reacting to the world.

My core beliefs are pro-union; but I am pragmatic in my thinking and approach. We must be willing to observe and analyze our conditions; and, like a bean counter (an accountant), become accountable to our industry and make the industry accountable to itself by educating, encouraging, and policing all who are in our industry.

This book will also discuss how to accept the truth and reason and react to it. It is not about idealism or wishing something was another way. As they say, the truth hurts and only the truth can set you free. This book is deliberate in its approach to attempt to get Unions and their respective Association leaders to look at things in a very uncomplicated and logical fashion. Our leaders usually tend to over-complicate things. They usually get too caught up in politics and posturing, and they usually over-think, then under-do, and frankly we, as the unionized sector, need a real action plan.

We will explore the reasons why we are fragmented as an industry, and how we need to change our standard if we are to ever attempt to retake command of our industry. We are going to look at the history of the construction unions and how the industry became fragmented, along with some of its problems stemming from fragmentation, and how it can be improved through a new business model and other approaches.

4

II. How the Industry Became Fragmented

If we were to look at the construction industry as a whole, it is over a $1-trillion industry in the United States alone. In fact, it is the single largest industry in the world; but as an industry, it has one major flaw: it is fragmented.

What do I mean by fragmented? Construction firms with a workforce of 10 employees and under, do 80% of all construction. Large and medium-size construction firms employing over 10 employees perform the remaining 20%. Now out of that 80%, firms employing fewer than 5 employees do approximately 63% and over of the construction. However, labor contracts and union business models do not reflect this truth or reality. Labor agreements as we know them now on a whole, were negotiated when unions were dominant in the industry, and reflect the truths, realities, and values of 40 years ago.

Fragmented: is this not exactly what the construction industry has become? We, as an industry, are not united in any way, shape, or form. Even the unions themselves are not united. Now, there are still pockets, or small areas where the union has a stronghold, but that is the exception, not the rule in today's economy.

Now let's discuss how the industry became this way. In the early turn of the 20th century, due to the Industrial Revolution, the United States and Canada went from an agricultural to industrial economy; therefore, providing new and innovative needs for both public and private sectors, customers/owners. The customers/owners at the turn of the century were usually large corporations, trusts (private), and government (public). Contractors (employers) were necessary to fill the demand of the customer. As a result of the capital requirements to perform for these large entities, there were only a handful of employers to provide the services needed by the customer.

When the building trade unions first formed, they were able to take advantage of the fact that there were a limited number of employers, making it relatively easy to organize a union within an employer. This is not to say that it was not a challenge for the founding fathers of unions. In fact, it was very difficult and required a great deal of sacrifice and bravery in the very early years. Nevertheless, with this small employer base, unions organized successfully since the industry was not fragmented.

The early union members formed unions, solely based on their word. In other words, their word was their bond. A simple handshake was the union agreement, along with the understanding that a union member would not work for less than another union member. This understanding became the foundation of the union movement, until formal apprenticeships came into existence.

These union members realized the realities of the marketplace for their time, and took realistic and deliberate risks for the circumstances they were in. They understood that uniting the industry was the only way to better themselves and the industry. As these unions grew, they were able to demand better wages and working conditions.

This eventually led to formal written labor agreements. The reason for formal written labor agreements was so the employer had a binding contract to avoid labor strife, at the whim of labor.

What you need to keep in mind is that technically during this period of time (the early 1900s), labor unions were not truly legitimate in the eyes of the government. And because of the informality of the union movement, the National Labor Relations Act (NLRA), also known as the Wagner Act, passed through Congress in the summer of 1935. It was put into place to legitimize and control the labor movement, and bring cohesion to both unions and employers in a formal and legal setting. This created ground rules for both unions and employers to abide by.

By legitimizing unions in the eyes of the government, it helped to bolster the union movement. In fact, by the 1950s and '60s, building trade unions became so successful and dominant that they controlled over 90% of the labor force in America. In addition, the majority of the contractor base in the construction industry was signatory to the union labor agreements as well. But as the unions kept demanding more and more wages, benefits, and conditions, there finally reached a breaking point for the customer/owner.

This is when the fragmentation of the industry started to have its effects on the unionized sector. With the urbanization and expansion of society, that handful of employers and customers that controlled the industry diminished, and eventually what used to be a handful of employers and customers/owners develop into hundreds of thousands of entities, which consequently changed the landscape of the construction industry to a fragmented industry.

When the larger customers/owners began to realize and study this trend, it gave rise to the non-union movement in construction as we now know it. Also during this same period, unions became overconfident as they dominated the industry. The unions believed they no longer had to organize, and started to restrict the ability of workers to join unions. When there was a labor shortage that the existing union membership could not fill, the unions dispatched under- or non-qualified manpower to the employers at full scale, but never took those employees into membership. Unions were no longer about banding together, but became country clubs and protectionist in their behavior.

Another phenomenon that was occurring was union members believed that certain types of work were beneath them, and hence the work was not manned. This created a vacuum that was seized upon by the non-union, or as some would say "open–shop" movement, led by such groups as the Associated Builders and Contractors (ABC). The non-union movement took advantage of the on-the-job training that the union gave to the under-skilled or non-qualified manpower that were never taken into union membership and who now had some skills.

An additional factor for this change in the union movement was that at this time in history, the union was comprised of the third and fourth generation union members. This generation of members was handed the union and never had to labor and sacrifice to create the union. They had an entitlement attitude, and a victim mentality, and believed the world owed them. Sacrifice was not in their vocabulary or belief. They were the arrogant offspring that got everything they wanted handed to them and never had to earn it. They did not know how to build a union they only understood what was given to them and expected that this was the way it always was and should be. So, when the construction landscape started to fragment, change for the labor movement was not an option in the mindset of the leadership at that time.

These new leaders of that time did not understand the nuances of the changes around them. They still were in the troughs of dominance and power. They did not understand that the customer/owner was looking for a more viable solution to its construction projects away from arrogance, strife, and complacency. The customer/owner wanted to buy what they wanted, not what the union told them they had to buy.

Now here we are today with about a 20 to 30 percent union market share; at least this is what I hear from the union labor leaders. I will tell you that it is much worse than this and our current union leaders and members are paying for the sins of their fathers. Now I am not going to blame our fathers for these sins, since it would be difficult for them to understand if they did not see it as a fragmenting problem.

The bottom line is we are living in a fragmented condition in the construction industry and everyone has their own agenda. Not only are we fighting the non-union movement, we are also fighting one union against another. The union movement as a whole is fragmenting and dissenting from within, with unions leaving the AFL/CIO and so on.

However, until we recognize this truth of a fragmented state of construction, we will never be able to better our industry. The unions need to reunite and look at its similarities, and not its differences.

We must remember that united we stand and divided we fall. We must set aside our differences and egos and unite our efforts to better our industry. But to do this, you need to realize that the whole industry is fragmented, and approach your organizing and business development efforts from this reality.

III. The Religion of Entitlement

I have to ask the question: are unions a religion of entitlement? To a majority in the union movement, unions are almost a form of religion. Many union members react with religious zeal when it comes to ideology they hold dear. They believe that it is an entitlement to have an 8-hour workday, healthcare benefits, pension benefits, etc…

The previously mentioned issues were hard-fought and won by our forefathers in the union movement, but as history always shows us, the competition is never over. Life does not stay stagnant, it is continually evolving. Either you take the challenge and continue to change and adapt or you lie down and get trampled by it. Now we must look at our current union movement conditions realistically. Labor unions in their infancy did not come to the bargaining table with entitlements. They came with economic issues that were relevant to their times, and grew those ideas as they became more prevalent in the industry. You cannot expect to demand something you do not have.

A union is not an entitlement organization it is an economic organization. We live in a capitalistic economy, not a socialistic economy. One of the many reasons for the decline in the union movement is that it has an entitlement approach to its positions. Unions have forgotten that they had to earn their achievements. It took blood, sweat, and sacrifice to get the labor movement to where it was a dominant force in the 1950s and '60s.

Now, because of our union forefathers' sacrifices, we in North America have been very privileged. We have been given opportunities that you would have never thought possible in other areas of the globe. What we consider poverty would be considered a rich man's life throughout most of the world. We are very fortunate and should thank God daily for what we have, and become appreciative of it.

Now, it's fine to have passionate zeal in the labor movement, but you must realize first and foremost that unions are an "economic service organization," a service business, and without the employer, your customer, you are just a club. You must always keep in mind that unions are only as successful as their signatory contractors, who are the employers, which is the union's customers. Learn to take the emotion out of your methodology, and learn to persuade your existing clientele and potential clientele that you are there to support them, and to help solve their problems and issues.

IV. Giving Away the Trade Secrets

Today we are living in an extremely competitive world and it gets more competitive every day. Those who hold the competitive advantage or trade secrets, rule the day; those who do not, get what's left.

What was the competitive advantage that the early unions had in the marketplace over their non-union counterparts? They held the trade secrets. Below are a few of those secrets that gave unions the advantage in the market place. It was what was attractive to the employee base during that time.

1) The eight-hour work day.
2) The forty-hour work week.
3) Overtime pay, time and one-half of regular pay after working an eight-hour shift.

The list could go on, but the above listed trade secrets were given to the government, federal, and state for no compensation.

The failure in the judgment of our union forefathers was they assumed that by giving the above listed issues to the government, the union would not have to bargain for these issues anymore because they were the law. What they did not realize by doing so was they had just given away their ability to have a competitive advantage in the marketplace. An employee no longer looked to the union for a better working environment; the government now held those secrets.

The failure of government is that the political party in power dictates what laws will be enforced. It is selective enforcement of the laws. If you hold the power then your issues or positions are enforced and the issues and positions that you do not champion are held at bay.

Now, you can get the government to abide by the law when you do not hold the keys to the power base, but it is up to you to round up all the evidence and substantiate it, and continually prod the bureaucrats to act in your behalf. It is not an effective way to make someone abide by the law, and it is one of the reasons why so many companies take advantage of the system.

I consider relying on the government as a means to buoy the union's position a mistake and an inefficient cost method to organizing and market share.

Project Labor Agreements (PLA's) have become the method of choice in the construction union movement as of late. I am not opposed to them, but you cannot rely on them to bolster your market, because it is a static market. PLA's are and should be just a tool in your tool-chest; by no means think that it is your complete toolbox solution. Once you think you have it as a given, you will be disappointed when the newly elected crowd that does not champion your ideas become the new power base in your area. Then out goes the PLA.

Remember that politics and government are fickle, and never consistent. You should be wary of trusting the government and/or politicians to champion your position—they will eventually bite you. They continually have to be bought off and stroked. If you had 90% of the contractor base signatory then there would be no need for PLA's, would there? Construction unions should focus on the ability to have, acquire, and retain signatory contractors and employers.

Now that we understand that we have given away our trade secrets, we now need to create new ones that will endear craft-workers and contractor/employers to the union movement.

V. The Force Factor

When the union movement was in its infancy, the employers of the day did not believe that their employees were of value. In fact, humanity as we now know it did not have a price tag of value. The world treated most workers no better than cattle. On the sum total, cattle were probably treated better than some humans previous to the union labor movement.

Creating the humanity and dignity that mankind should have in the work place is one of the reasons that the labor movement was born. In order to get the dignity and respect that mankind deserved, unions had to use what I like to call the force factor. Because the industry was virtually un-fragmented, the force factor or strike method, was the most effective means to gain a better way of life for the average worker in its day.

Strikes are a force factor way to show an employer your strength and resolve; and when there were just a few employers, the force factor worked and was effective.

For example, say there were only two plumbing contractors in town and between those two employers, they employed seventy craft-workers (employees). Now, if the union decides to strike one of those employers, what do you think will happen? First, the employer will most likely have self-preservation on his mind and will threaten to never employ the striking workers back, and will then try to hire replacement workers. By having this strike against an un-fragmented employer, you are able to put considerable pressure on the employer, especially if the union is able to stay in solidarity with each other and not cross the picket line and then is even more successful by being able to intimidate the possible replacement workers from crossing that line. Now that employer has a serious problem. If the employer is unable to get replacement workers, and if the buyer/owner, who is the employer's customer, is unable to secure a substitute contractor to replace the contractor, what happens?

If the only other contractor in town doesn't want to deal with his competitor's problem, what happens? There arise many questions that the employer must face. In this environment, the employer really has no choice but to negotiate a resolution with the union, since now the employer's self-preservation has had to change focus from replacing the work force to having no workforce to complete the project they are under contract with.

With an un-fragmented contractor base, as in the above example, it makes it very difficult for an employer not to negotiate with the union, especially if the union members have nearly complete solidarity among themselves.

Let's take another example. Say there were twenty-five plumbing contractors in town and between those twenty-five employers they employed seventy craft-workers. If the union decides to strike one of those employers, what do you think will happen? The possibility of the buyer/owner (the employer's customer) canceling the contract and replacing it with a new contractor is very likely. The likelihood of the employer replacing a few employees is also a real possibility since the intimidation factor of a few guys on the picket line is not that big of a deterrent for a hungry replacement worker. It is simply divide and conquer in the minds of the employer and the buyer/owner.

Because we currently are in a fragmented construction environment and in a "the customer is always right" mindset, we as a union sector have no choice but to change our force factor ways of thinking and reacting to our industry. No one, including unions, likes to be forced into making decisions, but this has been the union business methodology for quite some time, and it is not working in today's fragmented construction world. The intimidation force factor just keeps alienating the current contractor base, and keeps union market-share to a minimum in today's construction environment.

Again the buyer/owner knows he can shop his project to a multitude of contractors who are all too willing to compete for a business risk factor that has really only one major weak point and that is labor. Labor is the weakest and most volatile area to a contractor. If the employer can be non-union and keep his exposure to high wages and benefits at a minimum; have no burdensome labor conditions and force factor mindset employees; then that contractor or employer is reducing his exposure/risk factor. He then has a potential of making up for other inherent risks that coincide with the construction industry.

Business risk is the one thing that most union members and leaders never truly understand. I wish everyone in the construction industry could become a contractor/employer for at least one year and be willing to put their money, their home, and all they have on the line and risk it all. They would then understand, and hopefully appreciate, the position that the employer/ contractor has put himself into.

Again, we live in a fragmented construction environment. The average contractor/employer is a small business that usually has little to no financial resources and is typically unsophisticated in his business dealings. This average contractor/employer sees the union as a threat and not an asset; thus making the force factor or intimidation methodology an ineffective means to gain market share with the largest component of the marketplace -- the small contractor.

VI. The Spiraling Downward Theory

Today there is a whole generation or two who have had little to no experience with construction unions. That includes the customer or owner, the contractor, and the craft-workers/employees. This is because of what I call the spiraling downward theory.

When the average construction craft-worker decides to go into business for himself today, the thought of signing a collective bargaining agreement is not the first thing on his mind. In fact, it is probably the last thing on his mind, if it is on his mind at all. And why is that? Because the average new contractor has no business plan and no capital, he just wants to be a contractor for various reasons. The first and foremost reason is that he believes he will make more money by being a contractor, another reason is that he will have better security, etc.

Why would this craft-worker want to become a contractor? Usually he was working in an environment that was unsatisfactory: possibly non-union, low wages, no benefits or a combination of these. It is probable he wanted to better himself and felt this was the only way he could. So he becomes a contractor, and 99% of the time he is without any management experience or understanding of the inherent risks associated with contracting.

How does a new business get its customers in a competitive industry like construction? The new business must be willing to sell its services cheaper than its competition, or in other words it must steal the work away from a previous employer at a lower price. This is what I mean by spiraling downward, because the following generation will lower its price even more to steal the work away from its employer as well. This is why it is so difficult to sign a non-union employer. They know that as soon as they sign the agreement it means a death sentence for them, because they would eliminate the majority of the work they would be able to compete in.

In the beginning of this evolution to go to a non-union environment, the customer/owner was mainly concerned with union attitudes and working rules. Now that the non-union movement dominates the construction industry, the price of the product is usually the major factor. What we are currently living in is a low-bid world. What I like to call a Wal-Mart/McDonald's society, and again cost is the main reason.

Because of this ideology, our society has a tendency to push everything down to the lowest denominator, making it almost impossible for most start-up businesses to sign a collective bargaining agreement. The main reasons: the lack of viable capital of new contractors, the small rate of return on investment, and the certainty that the local union area/jurisdiction is typically not in command of its contractor base. All of which make it extremely difficult for a new contractor to become signatory and still be able to compete in the union market place under the typical union labor agreement.

Once more the fragmentation of the industry helps to keep this cycle of new contractors on the non-union side of the table. To correct this path, unions need to better understand its customers who are the contractors -- both signatory and non-signatory. The contractors' issues must be addressed if construction unions are to regain market share. It is imperative to understand what makes them tick and what makes them money and profit, and why. They are the construction union's only way to success.

It is imperative to stem the tide and realize and recognize the needs and concerns that a small business has, since they make up the majority of contractors. We can no longer approach our labor agreements as if they don't exist. They do, so let's deal with it.

With the natural attrition that occurs in the business cycle, we will be losing a majority of our current contractor base to the non-union through the attrition process, and I do not see a new method or wave of new union contractors coming into the marketplace to replace what we will lose over the next decade. Take the time and ask yourself how many union contractors have we lost over the last 40 years due to natural attrition? Then ask yourself how many union contractors have come in to replace the ones you have lost? The numbers will not be in the union's favor by a long margin.

The construction industry keeps growing every year but the union contractor base is becoming a relic in today's world; and along with that fact, the unions also are becoming relics as well.

Unions are intrinsically coupled to their employers; without an employer there is no union. If you learn nothing else from this book, please learn this simple truth -- unions without their employers are nothing but a social club. What empowers a union is its employers. This fact is the hardest pill for an ardent union member to understand.

Unions need employers (their customers) to survive. In view of the fact that the vast majority of the contractor base is small business (10 men and under) firms and smaller, construction unions need to reason and react to them as their bread and butter, because frankly they are. You need to get your collective bargaining agreements to become relevant to them. Once you do this, you will finally be on your way to selling your agreement to the existing non-union contractor base, your target client.

VII. An Old Approach to a Current Problem

Albert Einstein once said, "The definition of insanity is doing the same thing over and over again and expecting a different result."

The labor movement for the most part is doing exactly what Albert Einstein defined to be insanity. For the most part, unions promote leaders from within their own ranks, individuals who have given political favors, i.e., campaigned for, or actively recruited people for the union business manager's election.

The average union business manager has no business background. Most have no college degree, and most have never worked in management of any form before becoming business managers. As a result, the business manager becomes emotionally attached to the collective bargaining agreement during negotiations. This is where a lot of animosity with the contractor/employer comes into play. The union business manager is usually looking at the agreement from an emotional angle, not a logical one; and has the opinion, it used to be that way and it's going to stay that way. But the reality is nothing stays the same, and life is continually changing.

Union leadership is very political in its leadership ways of thinking. And because of this, union business managers usually look at things first politically and second logically; this is inclusive of union presidents and vice presidents as well. This hinders their ability to be effective leaders in today's fast-paced marketplace. This is one of the major reasons why unions are usually "too little, too late" in their economic stratagems.

An effective union president or business manager in today's world must be willing to do the correct thing, even if it costs him/her an election. They must be above the political pressure that resides in the international, regional, or local union, and make logical decisions based on the local market-share, economic conditions, etc., in its respective region. In other words, it must be gaining market-share, and signatory contractors and employers are the means to that end.

The old approach to unionism is not working for today's fragmented construction environment. The industry has problems that need to be addressed, analyzed, and followed through in a rational and non-emotional way. Where unions falter in today's marketplace is that they are usually emotionally, not logically involved in an issue.

Now, emotion is not a bad thing. In fact, it is a great motivating factor, and if it were not for emotion, you would typically never be able to get the rank and file to follow you. What union leaders usually do is to make their membership feel victimized. This gets the rank and file membership emotionally charged and willing to jump off a cliff with them. But playing the victim card is what is keeping unions from meeting their potential in a new and different world.

Unions are not victims and they need to start empowering their membership to this fact. Let's say that every contractor starting today were to sign the labor agreement. The existing union labor force could not meet the demands of the market.

The ability of the union labor movement in construction today, even if it wanted to, could not staff the work without accepting the current non-union labor forces with it.

Construction labor unions need to look at the fact that they are fortunate enough to have quality wages, benefits, and working conditions, which their non-union counterparts are not usually able to take advantage of. This is because they have union employers who generally have respect for them, and are willing to negotiate with the union who should represent the interests of the workforce.

The contractors who are currently signatory in today's environment choose to be, and unions need to respect and admire them for supporting unions in a fragmented and unfriendly to union environment. In fact, you should follow the words of your once great leader, Samuel Gompers, "Reward your friends, and punish your enemies." You as construction unions have to become friends with your customers, the employers, and truly partner with them. Then learn and practice the true meaning of win-win negotiating and partnering.

What is a true partner? Someone who is willing to risk, analyze, assess, understand, create, expand when needed, and downsize when needed. A partner is someone who understands that this life is not perfect, and that you must continually adapt to the new environments that this world gives you.

VIII. The Victimization of the Union Movement

Why is it that union leaders tend to portray to their memberships and potential members that they are victims of the employer? It's how they empower themselves as leaders. It is also propaganda to motivate the rank and file to do the will of the leaders. In fact Joseph Gerbals, Propaganda Minister of the Nazi Party in Germany, used victimization to motivate genocide. But what happens to victims? They eventually become helpless. And what becomes of people and individuals that become helpless? They become a burden on the backs of the individuals or organizations that support them. In other words, they become a drain on society.

It is no different than when an ambulance-chasing attorney whips you into a frenzy, telling you that you are the victim in an accident, then makes you believe that you deserve millions of dollars because someone may have caused an accident. They want to make you feel helpless and that you need them to punish the perpetrator. But what is the lawyer most interested in? The potential profit he will make off your suffering. Most accidents happen because they are simply accidents, not intentional incidents perpetrated by another party. The reality is that things happen in this world, which is perceived as unfair—so what! Is it fair that your neighbor gets cancer and you do not? Of course not, but that does not mean that the world is unfair. It just means you have to play the hand you are dealt. There has never been or ever will be a perfect contractor, employer, employee, etc. -- we all have short comings.

Do not complain and whine. Go do something that will make a positive change in the industry. Become a mentor to a young person, who is eager to go but is having difficulty with an aspect of your particular trade. Volunteer your time to help your union, or your trade, or your employer, and your industry. Be willing to sacrifice something that is dear to you for the betterment of the industry. Give a little extra every day to become the individual who is willing to always give 110% or more to the construction industry. Why? The construction industry is what feeds you.

Unions are not victims and neither are their memberships. In fact, the vast majority of union members are some of the brightest individuals I have met. But what drags this vast majority down is the minority of the membership that has become drains on their unions. In other words, they are the victimologists (study of victims) of the union movement. These individuals (victims) usually never take personal responsibility for their actions. When something does not go their way, they always point a finger at someone or something else. But these individuals want top dollar for their mediocre performance and services, making it tougher for the top-quality performers in the union movement to make the top dollar they rightfully deserve.

We live in an extremely competitive world today and in order to be the best, construction unions can no longer support mediocrity at full-scale. Construction unions need to become the most capable and skilled men and women in the industry. These men and women need to be problem solvers, willing to make things happen, not to just let things happen. Take charge and be responsible and accountable to your industry that provides you a living. Have a plan of action, and do not let your union just idle by. Know where you are headed, have a business plan and a guideline to go by, and then get involved in bringing about positive change.

IX. Ethical vs. Unethical

Which would you rather be, ethical or unethical? The problem we have in this world is that what is ethical to one individual or group would be considered unethical to another individual or group. So who is right? In our society, we have the rule of law and we should respect it; because without it you have chaos. In any society you will have individuals, groups or organizations that are law abiding and non-law abiding. Just because something is the law, it does not necessarily translate to being ethical to everyone in the society.

Is it unethical to be a non-union employer? To those who champion the union movement it is; but to those employers and individuals who do not champion the union movement, to them they believe they have the ethical high ground. This makes for quite the dilemma, who is correct?

Now, if you feel a law is unethical then you as an individual or group must do your part to change or enact the law to meet your definition of ethical. The reality is that there are both ethical and unethical contractors/employers, owners, employees, politicians, bureaucrats, etc. What really matters is the law in our society, but the problem is some laws are enforced while other laws are not, because as a society we are an "enforcement by convenience" society. Those who are holding the power at the moment tend to enforce the laws that they deem ethical.

So what is ethical? Really what is ethical is what the law is. So part of your business plan must speak to the law and the enforcement of it for the betterment of the construction industry. In the construction industry, the willingness to let the unethical or law breakers survive and thrive makes it harder and less profitable on the ethical or law abiders.

For example, there are laws that make an employer provide workers compensation insurance for its employees (ethical). Do all employers provide this? Of course not, some have chosen not to (unethical). So this puts a larger financial burden on the ethical ones that do.

Ask yourself this question: would you prefer to work for an unethical union employer, or an ethical non-union employer? For the true-blue, die-in-the-wool union craft-worker, I would have to say 99% of the time they would answer in favor of the unethical union employer, and why? Because the overall value system is of the same mindset. Again we must ask ourselves, what is our value system for ethics? We need to turn aside from our perceived view of ethical and then ask questions as to legality, since that is where we will be able to truly make a difference. If you are going to argue from ethics, it must be founded in law. If you feel that something is unethical, then you must enact it into law before it can be argued as ethical.

Let's look at another question regarding ethics: do you believe prevailing wages or the Davis/Bacon Act are ethical? To many in the country, their core beliefs are that this is an unethical issue, but the reality is that it is ethical, and why? Because it is the law, and the law in our society governs what is ethical and what is not.

So my petition to the whole construction industry is that we need to be willing to enforce the law in our industry and be willing to police and take legal action on those who do not abide the law -- the truly unethical.

So, how does this ethical-unethical thing apply to the construction unions? Union members may feel very strongly about the non-union contractor/employer being unethical in their viewpoint, but as a matter of law, it is ethical because it is legal to be a non-union employer.

Now, I have been in bottom-up organizing campaigns where the employer told me that what I was doing by trying to recruit his employees to join the union was unethical; however, the fact is -- it is ethical because it is legal. It doesn't really matter how the employer feels about the organizing issue, it is the law, and therefore ethical in our society. Now, that doesn't mean that the employer likes the law or cannot try to enact his version of ethics into law. Nevertheless, until his version is enacted into law, the right to organize a union is therefore legal and ethical.

What is the most efficient way of finding out whether a non-union employer is abiding by the law or not? It is to salt the employer and gather data and information. We, as a union construction industry, should be willing as members to police our industry, and then start putting the pressure on the law-breakers in our industry. That should also involve those employees who abuse the workers' compensation laws, the unemployment compensation laws, and other issues as well.

As an industry, we need to tolerate only ethical or legal behavior and enact laws necessary to help the enforcement of the ethics that are needed in our industry. We need to weed out the contractors and craft-workers who are unethical and do not abide the law. They are just a drain and create an unnecessary burden to our industry.

X. Understanding the Contractor's World

Now that you know the history of the union and some of its problems, it's important to understand the world of the contractor. There are three types of contractors:

1. Signatory Contractors: these are employers who are already in your market-share and should be cared for so they remain your clients.
2. The Non-Union Contractor: these employers are non-signatory for various reasons and are your potential client base.
3. The Anti-Union Contractor: usually this contractor has a philosophical difference that you will, 99% of the time, never be able to overcome in an organizing/business development marketing plan.

The signatory contractors are your current client base and they need to become appreciated and coddled. They need to know that you, the construction union, understand their concerns and are willing to adapt and accommodate their individual business issues. Remember, these are your steady clients learn to, as Samuel Gompers says, "reward your friends" because that is exactly what they are, your friends. In reality, they could have left the collective bargaining agreements years ago and there is a reason why they have not. Learn those reasons, support their needs and assist them to be better and more productive contractors/employers. Encourage them to grow and create ways for them to be able to take more calculated risks.

The Non-Union Contractors are employers who happen to be non-signatory for various reasons. This is your potential new client base and the necessary means in which to grow your union. You must come to know this clientele and meet or exceed their needs. These employers need to be approached top-down for the most part, but you had better have a product that the non-union employers can buy into. If you do not, you are wasting their time and yours as well. Develop your collective bargaining agreement to meet their needs and you will be able to sign them.

The Anti-Union Contractors are the employers who have no regard for your beliefs or needs as a union. These employers have an at-war mentality with the union movement and have a religious zeal and philosophical difference with your organization. For the most part you must, as Samuel Gompers says, "punish your enemies." These employers need to be approached primarily from a bottom-up method. These employers are willing to go to war with you, and you must be prepared for that to possibly happen. This type of contractor is usually emotionally attached to his anti-union philosophy, and if you can exploit his emotionality, he will cease to be able to reason like a business should.

On the whole, today's average contractor is a one-man operation that employs five or fewer craft-workers in the field. He works out of his garage with the belief that he has no overhead.

The strengths of this average contractor are his ability to sell his services one-on-one and to have a true personal relationship with his customers. He is usually a self-starter and hard worker, willing to do whatever it takes to get the job done. From an economic standpoint in the competitive bidding world, this contractor has the leg up on the low bid, since he is willing to work for wages. This average contractor is usually a hands-on craftsman working with the tools about 90% or more of the time.

The weaknesses of this average contractor are: he is usually less educated, under capitalized, and typically less organized. His grasp of lien laws, contract law, employment laws, accounting principles, estimating essentials, etc., is usually weak. This average contractor is much more willing to take the risk of a handshake contract over a written contract. This contractor usually never worries with labor laws, and frankly is not too concerned with them either. His labor force is usually a friend or an acquaintance that will work under the table, a day laborer hired off the street and paid cash, or a temp hired through a temp hire agency. He usually does not keep accurate accounting and bookkeeping records. This average contractor 99% of the time is non-union and makes up approximately 50% on the available contractor base.

Before unions will ever reclaim the market in a fragmented construction environment, they must come to understand the world of a contractor. The success of construction unions rests solely on the success of the contractors/employers. This is a very hard concept for most union members and leaders to grasp, but the union that is willing to embrace this concept will flourish in this fragmented state of construction.

Unions at their core cannot exist without employers. However, employers can exist without unions. This is why a new business model and plan is crucial to construction union's survival and existence. It is the primary reason why you must understand the world of the contractor.

The world of the contractor today is in a constant state of risk: from litigation, cash flow difficulty, small return on investment (ROI), workers' compensation insurance worries, quality labor issues, labor training, management education, and material escalations, just to name a few. Labor is but one of the many considerations that is on the mind of the contractor. Let me reiterate that -- labor is but one of the many considerations on the mind of the contractor.

Now, labor would love to believe that the only consideration in a contractor's mind is labor, but this is not the case. If the union's labor costs, conditions, and attitudes keep pushing union contractors out of their ability to secure construction projects, then as a business the employers have to look at other alternatives in order to survive, and this is exactly what they have been doing. Remember unions are not the only game in town. Contractors of today are risk managers, and if the union is perceived as any kind of a threat, they will drop you like the plague, and want nothing to do with you or your organization. Contractors are problem solvers, and if your organization is not of the same mindset, then you are not going to win them over.

With the competitive bid world in which contractors live, there leaves little room for error and since contractors provide "estimates" and not "exactments," this means inherent risk.

There is nothing exact in construction, and contractors are subject to a great deal of risk when they sign a construction contract. Now, if that construction contract requires a bond, you have just added even more personal risk to the contractor, since as a small contractor you are usually using your personal home as the collateral for the bond. Can you see what a great deal of risk the contractor is taking? If the contractor were to go belly up on the job, not only is he losing his business, he is going to lose his home as well.

You must understand that the contractor is responsible for completing the construction contract period, even when he has lost his shirt on the job. Somehow construction unions have to become more grateful for the position the contractor is willing to put himself into, seeing that without that risk-taking contractor, you, the craft-worker, have no job.

Let's discuss the estimating process and how that affects the contractor, which in turn affects the construction union. The contractor has to meet at least two bottom lines in order to stay in business.

The estimator's table is where all the deals are cut, and if an estimator cannot obtain work, the business will cease to exist. That is the first bottom line the contractor has to face to stay in business. This is a double-edged sword because once the estimator/contractor secures the estimate, the contractor must now prove he is capable of performing the installation to meet or exceed the estimator's budget. This is now the second bottom line a contractor must meet. Now let's discuss what an estimate is.

What is an estimate? It is an educated guess as to what a project will cost, and what the market will bear as to a markup to those costs. In fact, it is a budget that makes assumptions as to what material, labor, equipment, sub-contracts, etc., will cost so as to be able to make a profit at a certain mark-up.

What usually happens with construction projects is that they are bid today with today's cost and mark-ups. But then those projects are usually not started until six or more months down the road, and do not take into consideration any inflation in the industry. This means that what you budgeted for the project is now subjected to the whims of inflation.

If you have signed the contract within a few weeks or months of the quote, the longer it takes to start the actual construction will keep pushing you into a less and less profitable position.

If you are fortunate enough to not sign a contract within a few weeks of the quote, then you are in a more favorable position to negotiate the additional cost of inflation. But this does not always mean that you will be successful at doing so.

Let's look at the following example: Table #1 is a typical method of budgeting an estimate for the average subcontractor.

TABLE # 1

Construction Estimate		Estimated Budget
Material		$50,000
Taxes on Material	7.75%	$3,875
Total Material Costs		$53,875
Labor		$30,800
Labor Burden	24.00%	$7,392
Labor Fringes	52.00%	$16,016
Total Labor Costs		$54,208
Equipment Costs		$5,674
Direct Job Costs		$1,915
Sub-Contracts		$10,808
Sub Total (Prime Costs)		$126,481
Overhead & Profit Mark-Up	20.00%	$25,296
Total Estimate		$151,777

The table above is not complicated and the average person should be able to understand it. The previous Table #1 is the reference point in which the contractor starts a project. This budget, alone in a perfect world, the contractor would be able to make a profit. But what do we, as practical construction hands, know about construction? It is full of pitfalls, such as stacking of trades, confined environments, other subcontractors not performing to schedule, field employees not performing to expectations, management employees not performing to the needs of the field, inspection authorities' interpretations of codes, general contractor or owner not paying in a timely manner, the list could go on and on.

Now let's look at the following example: We will make the assumption that Table #1 is our original estimate, in which the contractor bid the work. Now the contractor is awarded the contract, but the start of construction is delayed nine months.

During those nine months, inflation has kicked in and material prices have increased 25%, labor costs have increased 5%, equipment costs have increased 10%, and direct job costs have increased 6%.

Since the contractor has a contract for the original estimate based on the budget in Table #1, the contractor is bound by law to complete it for the contract amount of $151,777.00. The owner really doesn't care that the inflation in construction costs has occurred. The owner knows that he has a contract at a stated price and it is the contractor's duty to perform to the contract's language and to complete the contract at the original affirmed contract price.

As you can see in the following Table # 2, before the contractor ever started to mobilize on the job, he has already lost $16,680.00 dollars. To make up this lost dollar amount, the contractor will now have to try and make it up in his labor costs because that is the only area that he can truly squeeze. Again, labor is the riskiest area that the contractor/employer has in a project. It is just full of pitfalls and risks and must be managed well to be efficient.

This means that the contractor is going to have to try and cut almost 30% out of his labor budget. In other words, he needs to be at least 30% more efficient in his labor to make up that difference, in order to keep with his original overhead and profit mark-up budget of $25,296. Is 30% a reasonable amount of efficacy? As we all know, most likely the contractor will never be able to make this 30% loss up in labor only. You can see the detail in the following Table #2.

TABLE # 2

Construction Budget vs. Actual Budget		Original Estimate Budget	New Budget due to Inflation Costs	Cost Variance
Material		$50,000	$62,500	($12,500)
Taxes on Material	7.75%	$3,875	$4,844	($969)
Total Material Costs		$53,875	$67,344	($13,469)
Labor		$30,800	$32,340	($1,540)
Labor Burden	24.00%	$7,392	$7,762	($370)
Labor Fringes	52.00%	$16,016	$16,817	($801)
Total Labor Costs		$54,208	$56,918	($2,710)
Equipment Costs		$5,674	$6,241	($567)
Direct Job Costs		$1,915	$2,030	($115)
Sub-Contracts		$10,808	$10,808	$0
Sub Total (Prime Costs)		$126,481	$143,341	$143,341
Overhead & Profit Mark-Up	20.00%	$25,296		$8,436
Totals		**$151,777**	$151,777	$151,777

Now, the aforementioned is just a sample of situations that a contractor/employer puts himself at risk with just to operate a business everyday. It's not for the weak, and it should also not be for the uneducated, or unethical. But the current fragmented construction industry is full of them, the uneducated and the unethical.

Now, as an industry we need to better police and educate our industry.

XI. The Transitional Workforce

What is one of the biggest factors killing the union construction movement? The transitional workforce.

What is the transitional workforce? It is the unskilled craft-workers who start to work in construction, but within a few months or years realize this industry is not cut out for them. It is what makes the non-union viable in the marketplace. It is also what the traditional union membership and leadership fear most. This current transitional workforce comes into the construction industry because it's usually fairly easy to find employment since we are a fragmented industry, and the transitional workforce doesn't quite know what it wants to do in life yet. The vast majority stays in the construction trades only about one to three years and then moves on to another line of work. Unions are not using this workforce reality to their advantage because of their traditions and mindsets that restrict them from being innovative.

How did the construction unions originally handle labor shortages after they dominated the market and put restrictions on union membership? They used unskilled labor at full scale and then never made them members of the union. We all know that the vast majority of the union pay scales are pretty darn good wages in our economy. So when there was no more work available, you released these once unskilled workers into the marketplace, now having some skills that they were able to acquire over the last few years being in the industry, and on top of that they were now used to being paid full scale. Do you think that this transitional worker is now going to leave the trade? Of course not, you spoiled him with your high wage scale. And even if he is only going to be paid 60% to 70% of what the union scale is while working non-union, he won't notice it because around 40% of union scale is benefits that he never sees on the check anyway.

Now, because of our infrastructure in the union construction arena, we have the journeyman and the apprentice as our working models. The journeyman is supposedly skilled, the apprentice is supposedly unskilled to semiskilled and learning the skills of the trade. Yet we only accept a small portion of apprentices into our union apprenticeships every year. When the contractor needs additional unskilled labor, the union contractor has nowhere to get the additional unskilled workers. So he has to hire the journeyman to handle most of the unskilled and semi-skilled work, which in today's economy is not cost effective and therefore pushes the unionized construction method out of the ballpark in the vast majority of the construction market.

This transitional workforce is the means to getting the job done in a cost-effective manner. In today's economy, there are more plug-and-play materials that are being installed on the job. Since this is the truth, a contractor does not need the vast majority of his workforce to be skilled. What today's construction industry is using are more skilled or refined specialists, who are supervising the unskilled and semiskilled, which are the bulk of the workers in construction today. This is exactly what the non-union contractors are doing, and because the unions have refused to accept that the industry is changing, they have lost their foothold on the market. We in the union movement are so caught up in the wage structure of the journeyman that we have ignored the realities and changes in the construction installation methodology of having more prefabricated products to install on the job.

The reality is the innovators will always rule the day, and if the construction unions do not embrace innovation, then don't complain that you have lost market-share. Now, that doesn't necessarily mean that you like the innovative method. In fact, you might think it's completely ridiculous; but it doesn't mean that you bow your back and not accept it, because the individual that does accept innovation has the installation advantage over you. We live in a competitive world—get used to it, embrace it, and accept it.

Construction unions, we need to change our traditional working model of the journeyman, and the apprentice. We, as construction unions, need to come to grips with the notion that "I will not work for less than union scale unless I am an apprentice," since unions have no union solidarity in the majority of the workforce. Besides, if you are willing to pay someone less than scale to be an apprentice, why would you pay an unskilled transitional worker full union scale when you have run out of apprentices. It's not fair to the apprentice or the industry.

Our new working model should become the journeyman, the apprentice and the transitional worker: helper, grunt, pre-apprentice, or whatever name you would like to insert. Now here is my argument to make the above new working model part of our official change to our traditional paradigm, and to incorporate it into our new union business model.

There are actually three types of workers required on a construction project in today's marketplace.

1. Journeyman: skilled level or above to handle the complicated issues and have the expertise to solve the issues.
2. Apprentice: semi-skilled level to handle the semi-skilled issues on a project, who can think through most issues on their own but needs assistance and training.
3. Transitional worker: unskilled level who can handle mundane and unskilled issues, and hopefully will try to move up to the apprentice level once he finds out whether or not the construction trades are cut out for him.

In the traditional approach of the union apprenticeship, we are bringing in workers who are typically unskilled. We also do not know their work ethic, absentee habits, tardiness habits, and etc. Now on top of that, we pay them way too much money as a first period apprentice to figure this out. In my trade as an electrical contractor in Riverside County, California, a first period 40% apprentice makes about $13.00 per hour on the check plus benefits which costs the contractor/employer around $24.50 per hour in total costs. That is a substantial amount of money to pay someone with no track record in any industry, and I do not know of any other industry that starts its unskilled labor force off at that high rate of compensation and costs.

By having the transitional worker (helper, grunt, pre-apprentice, etc.) in your working portfolio, or model, you are able to kill multiple birds with one stone. You are able to

A gift note from
Glenn G De Soto:

Bill, It was great meeting you, I hope you enjoy the book and we will have to have lunch and once you have read it. Glenn De Soto

Included with Fragmented, the Demise of Unionized Construction

ınopened or original
e your order ID ready.

amazon.com

**Glenn G De Soto
has sent you a gift.**

Your order of February 9, 2012 (Order ID 002-5874252-2901052)

Qty.	Item
1	**Fragmented, the Demise of Unionized Construction** G., Glenn De --- Paperback **(** ** C-5 -- T-3-901 ** **) 1847285775**

This completes your gift order.

Have feedback on how we packaged your order? Tell us at www.amazon.com/packa

Returns Are Easy!

Visit http://www.amazon.com/returns to return any item - including gifts -
condition within 30 days for a full refund (other restrictions apply). Please k

make the union contractor more competitive. At the same time, you are able to evaluate a potential apprentice and determine his value to possibly take to the next level, which is the apprenticeship. Now by taking this approach, your apprentice has more working skills when he enters the apprenticeship, and is therefore more productive for your industry.

Let's look at the following Table # 3.

TABLE #3

Five Craft-Worker Crew	Unit	Per Hour Costs
Standard Crew	5	$220
Journeyman	3	$50
Apprentice	2	$35
Transitional Crew	5	$148
Journeyman	1	$50
Apprentice	2	$35
Transitional Worker	2	$14

In the above table, we have a standard five craft-worker crew of 3 journeyman and 2 apprentices, which is a fairly standard crew mix in a union environment. The total crew costs per hour for the standard crew are $220.00 per hour.

Also in the above table, we have a new crew called the transitional crew made up of five craft-workers of 1 journeyman, 2 apprentices, and 2 transitional workers. The total crew costs per hour for the transitional crew are $148.00 per hour.

By using the transition crew mix, a contractor/employer can be more cost efficient and therefore more competitive in the marketplace. With a standard crew, you would have to be 33% more efficient in costs, meaning that if a job were to take 200 man-hours, the standard crew would have to be able to perform at 134 man-hours to equal the same costs as the transitional crew. Do you believe that your union workforce with its standard crew mix can perform every day at 33% more efficiency? I will tell you -- it cannot. That's not to say that on a given day you couldn't beat the odds; but to consistently day in and day out, perform at least 33% more efficiently than the transitional crew is not a reality. This is the major reason the non-union is winning in the market place. On any given project, the non-union contractor/employer are between 30% to 50% more cost effective than the union contractor/employer is able to be because of our current crew mix.

Let's look at the following Table #4 in regards to a standard crew mix.

TABLE #4

Standard Crew Mix				
Total Project Man-hours		200		
Skill Level	**Percentage of Efficiency**	**Man-hours Required**	**Journ.**	**Appr.**
skilled-technical	20%	40	40	
semi-skilled and technical	30%	60	60	
unskilled and non-technical	50%	100	20	80

The above Table # 4 is an example of a project with 200 projected man-hours. The type of project requires a certain percentage of skill levels. You can see right away that the required skill levels are not being used efficiently. The skilled work is being staffed at 100% efficiency. The semi-skilled worker is being staffed 100% by over-skilled workers, causing an undue burden on costs as they relate to the requirements of the job. The unskilled work is also being staffed 100% by over-skilled workers, again causing an undue burden on the costs of the project.

Let's look at the following Table #5 in regards to a transitional crew mix.

TABLE #5

Transitional Crew Mix					
Total Project Man-hours		200			
Skill Level	**Percentage of Efficiency**	**Man-hours Required**	**Journ.**	**Appr.**	**Trans.**
skilled-technical	20%	40	40		
semi-skilled and technical	30%	60		60	
unskilled and non-technical	50%	100		20	80

The above Table # 5 is an example of this same project but with a transitional crew mix. You can see right away that the required skill levels are being used much more efficiently. The skilled work is being staffed at 100% efficiency. The semi-skilled work is being staffed at 100% efficiency, while the unskilled work is being staffed at 80% efficiency. The biggest key factor is that you are not using journeymen to staff semi-skilled and unskilled work, which keeps your cost down and makes the union more viable in the marketplace of today.

The truth is that in construction you will never truly be able to be 100% efficient, but being 90% is better than being 50%. Every project will require a different percentage of skill level sets, but the average project in today's world would reflect the percentage of efficiency shown in Tables 4 and 5.

What is the biggest advantage to having a transitional worker classification in your mix? The vast majority of the workforces in construction today are individuals who are trying to find out what they want to do with themselves. By utilizing this worker base, you are able to be more cost efficient, and you are also not keeping individuals who do not really have their hearts set on being in this industry; individuals who stay in the industry only because of the high union wages. By utilizing this worker base, you are also able to evaluate personnel as to absenteeism, tardiness, work ethics, or simply, are they cut out for the demands of this industry? Also by utilizing this worker base efficiently and observing and monitoring these individuals, you will have better apprentices in your apprenticeship programs, since you are able to weed out those candidates who are not committed to excellence, which is what we as a unionized sector need.

XI. THE TRANSITIONAL WORKFORCE

Some of the construction unions have already started commitment to excellence programs which are extremely needed avenues to position your business plan into success. It is a commitment to this industry that we need to be the best, and to be the best means that you are using all cylinders and avenues to perform to your peak performance. And in order to do that and to be competitive, you must be willing and prepared to accept the reality that the majority of the construction work force in today's economy is a transitional worker, someone who is using this industry as a means to find themselves and determine whether they will fit into this industry or not.

XII. The Business Model of Union Organizing

Now that we have discussed the contractor's world and the current status of the work force, it is time to explain the current business model of the union. Then we will introduce a new business model.

Construction union leaders are probably saying to themselves right now, "a business model? We are not a business." Oh! But you are. You just haven't realized it yet.

From the conception of unionization to the present, the same union business model for organizing has basically been used, with a few minor variations here or there. The union business model is an adversarial relationship with the employer. The model was based on intimidation, with strikes being the primary intimidation method.

The adversarial relationship was logical for the early days of unions, based on labor conditions at that time in history. And because of the truth that the industry was virtually un-fragmented, this form of relationship worked. This was also due to the fact that there were only a handful of employers during the early days of the union movement, and the union business model was effective for its time.

As time went by, unions and employers were able to benefit from this business model when the unions dominated the industry and the industry was less fragmented. During that period, the employer used the union in a "good cop, bad cop" method to sell its services to the customer, and to make a substantial profit. For example, when the customer/owner complained of the high cost and conditions of a contract with the employer, the employer would claim that unions were in such control of the work force that there were virtually no options for the customer, and that was the truth and reality of the marketplace at that time.

This approach to the industry worked for decades, but created a wedge in the outlook of the customer/owner about the union movement. The unions fell into classic overconfidence that comes from having too much power, and believed they were untouchable. Instead of constantly observing and studying the economic trends, labor unions at that time really believed that an employer would not be able to survive without them. The arrogant union members of that period forgot that there had been employers in this world for centuries and millenniums before unions ever came into existence or power. Unions forgot that this union movement was quite unique in the history of this world, and did not have much of a track record to boot.

Once the leadership of the construction unions finally realized that they had a problem and were losing membership, they also noticed that their market share was completely eroding. They tried to prevent this consequence, but did not study the underlying affects of why they were eroding. The remedies they tried were usually just band-aids on the larger problem that they could not see: fragmentation of the construction industry.

Construction unions still seemed to think that the employer would/could not exist without them, and were not looking at why contractors and owners were leaving the collective bargaining agreements. They tried new avenues with little to no success.

Programs like market recovery (union members paying higher dues to be given back to a contractor who was bidding work so as to not cut the overall wage base) were instituted to try and keep the status quo, while attempting to be competitive. This program was initiated with the idea that the Union would be in control of the projects they were willing to deem as lost markets, while not understanding what their market really was.

Labor Management Cooperative Committees (LMCC's) were instituted to get management and labor to communicate in a bipartisanship fashion. They were designed to keep a dialog and a spirit of cooperation going between labor agreement terms.

Bottom-up union organizing was re-instituted to try to persuade non-union employees to become union and to try to create an Unfair Labor Practice (ULP) on the employers who violated a union member's rights under the law to organize.

All of these efforts taken one by one are good ideas, but unions were never looking at the fragmented state that the construction industry is in. Because of the "us against them" ways of dealing with our times and conditions, we (union) are continually putting wedges into our union business plan that are not effective for our current and future market conditions.

Also temporary hiring services, i.e. Manpower, Contractors Labor Pool, etc. have stolen part of the construction unions business model by having a craft-worker referral service, but with no real strings attached. What construction unions are perceived as in today's economy, are a temp service with attitude, and plenty of restrictive strings attached. Construction unions are not seen as a human resource department, like their counter-parts the temporary hiring services, which is what the construction unions should be.

Now, for construction unions to survive, the business model of construction unions must change to reflect the current fragmented conditions of the construction industry. If unions don't change, they will become irrelevant to the marketplace. In fact, in the majority of the economy, construction unions no longer have a role because of the traditions and business models they hold dear.

Union members need to ask themselves this question: As a union member or leader, where as an organization will we/I be in the market share conditions in five years? If you cannot answer that question in an effective manner, then you need to start today to organize and formulate a business plan and model that will get you more market share and create the ability to further your influence in the industry. I can tell you that a majority of the construction unions have no idea of where they will be in five years. If you have no plan then you will never be able to focus your desires for a better unionized construction atmosphere.

As a signatory or potential signatory employer, why would I want to partner with your organization, knowing that you have no real business plan for your future? Where is your vision, where is your plan of action to recapture the market? If you are only concerned with status quo, and that status quo is to keep dying on the vine, then as a contractor/employer or should I say partner, what is the benefit for me, the contractor/employer, to sign on with you, the union?

Take a good look at your construction union organization and ask yourself: are unions benefiting the marketplace by being in the minority because we do not want to change our status quo mindset? I will tell you, no! Because if you are not in the market, you cannot influence the market—it's that simple.

The world and economy is constantly changing and if unions are not able to adapt and change with it, they --like the dinosaurs -- will become extinct, and unions already are an endangered species.

A constructive business model and plan is the first step to the start of your transformation: to go from being the exception method of construction to becoming the standard method of construction.

XIII. The New Construction Union Business Model and Plan

Construction unions must create a business model that will reflect the ability to generate revenue and be self-sustaining or to make a profit. The business model should also include the transitional worker in the crew mix, and customer (contractor/employer) services should be the statement of belief. In other words, the construction union is recognizing that it is a service business and organization.

Let's discuss what a service is, and realize that not only is the construction union providing a service to the contractor, but the contractor is also a service business providing a service to the customer/owner.

In economics and marketing, a service is the non-material equivalent of goods. Service provision has been defined as an economic activity that does not result in ownership and this is what differentiates it from providing physical goods. It is claimed to be a process that creates benefits by facilitating a change in customers, a change in their physical possessions or a change in their intangible assets. This is done by supplying some level of skill, ingenuity, and experience. Providers of a service participate in an economy without the restrictions of carrying stock (inventory) or the need to concern themselves with bulky raw materials. On the other hand, the investment in expertise does require marketing and upgrading (continual education) in the face of competition which has equally few physical restrictions.

Service providers (construction unions) face obstacles selling services that goods-sellers rarely face. Services are not tangible, making it difficult for potential customers to understand what they will receive and what value that service will hold for them. Indeed some services, such as consulting and investment services, along with construction unions, offer no guarantees of the value for price paid.

Since the quality of most services depends largely on the quality of the individuals providing the services, in this case the individual union member, it is true that "people costs" are a high component of service costs. Whereas a manufacturer may use technology, simplification, and other techniques to lower the cost of goods sold, the service provider often faces an unrelenting pattern of increasing costs.

Differentiation is often difficult. How does one customer/owner choose one service over another (union vs. non-union), since they often seem to provide identical services? Charging a premium for services is usually an option only for the most established firms who are able to charge extra based upon brand recognition and a proven track record. But in the competitive bid economy, and in the minds of the average customer/owner, price is the determining factor, or a perceived value since the service is perceived to be the same whether union or non-union.

Service provider operations are intended to produce services that are intended for customers/owners who determine the value of those services through their desire to buy them or not, and through the prices that they are willing to pay for those services. Service businesses/construction unions should respond to the customers'/employers' desires by putting in place a set of operations or a relevant collective bargaining agreement that enables the contractors/employers to produce and deliver their productivity to the end user, the customer/owner.

Let's discuss what a value chain is as it relates to a construction union. The processes that make it possible for the business/organization (union) to put out services (craft-workers) intended for their customers (contractors/employers) are called a value chain. Analysis of the business/organization (construction union) value chain helps trace the flow of the service (craft-workers) transformation from beginning to end. For a lean-oriented organization, the service process should be set in such a way that at every step of the process, value is expected to be added to the service being provided to the end user (customer/owner).

Waste (disruptive or under-skilled for the position craft-workers) occurs every time the material/service goes through a step without having value added to it and every time it is stored at a given stage of the process waiting to be further transformed.

Even though it is more obvious in manufacturing settings, this concept also applies to services. Business (construction union) organizational structures are composed of several departments (individual union members) that put in place distinct processes (craft-worker skill sets) and those departments operate in contingent sequences with different operations at different stages and areas of the organization being dependent on each other (union and employer).

Because of this interdependence of the different operations, every time a process at a given department (individual union member) fails to operate to its full potential or conflicts with other departments, it becomes a constraint, or a bottleneck for the business/organization and contractor (union and employer) as an entity. The good performance of each department only positively impacts the business/organization (union) as an entity when every department (individual union member) performs to its full potential and does not constitute a hindrance or a constraint for the rest of the company (employer) or organization (union).

What are some of the best values (services) that a construction union has to offer currently?

1. Craft-worker referral service.
2. Training service.
3. An established pension and health and welfare system.
4. A network of professional craft-workers.
5. In most cases a LMCC (Labor Management Cooperative Committee).

How can you, the construction union organization, give added value/ services to attract additional clients?

1. Flexible work rules.
2. More competitive crew mixes.
3. A Visa/ATM card for all craft-workers to alleviate getting paychecks to job sites, like many of the temp services are using.

4. Extended warranty programs for your union craft-worker services.
5. A one-day no cost obligation to the employer when you, the union, refers an unknown craft-worker to the employer.

There are thousands of ideas and services that can be of added value to a contractor/employer that you will have to look at and include in your business plan.

Now, let's discuss what a business plan is. In order to attract capital (investors/membership) into a business/organization, there needs to be a viable document called the Business Plan. In order to have a detailed business plan, you will need to follow the suggested outline that is inclusive of the following:

1. **Executive Summary**: an overview of the main points of a business plan or proposal.
    a. **Plan Objectives**: something worked toward or striven for; a goal, in other words where are you going?
    b. **Mission Statement**: a summary describing the aims, values, and overall plan of the organization.
    c. **Keys to Success**: describe how your services will be developed and provided; have follow-up strategies to gauge performance with clients, along with the implementation and maintenance of a quality control and assurance policy.
2. **Company/Organization Summary**: a definition of what you will be providing, such as services for clients, or markets such as residential, commercial,

and industrial, also where your energies will be focused.

    a. **Company/Organization Ownership**: who will own the company/organization, i.e. union membership.

    b. **Start-up Summary**: describe the initial costs, requirements, equipment, licensing, etc., associated with the implementation of the new plan.

    c. **Company/Organization Locations and Facilities**: describe the location of the business/organization, the size of the facility required, what communication systems you will have, and if you will host a Web site, etc.

3. **Services**: describe the services you will be providing, the markets where you will be providing those services, i.e., residential, commercial, industrial, etc., and if innovative and economical services will be offered; also whether clients' needs will be met on projects of all sizes or not.

    a. **Service Description**: a breakdown of all the services you will provide, with a brief description highlighting each service.

    b. **Competitive Comparison**: describe the advantages of using your services rather than any others available.

    c. **Marketing & Sales Literature**: describe the method of literature and means to market your services.

    d. **Fulfillment**: describe how you will fulfill the Business Plan, and by what means, and on what timeline.

      e. **Technology**: describe the technologies that will be used to fulfill your Business Plan.

      f. **Future Services**: describe the future services that you will provide.

4. **Market Analysis Summary**: give a brief description of the market you are in and how that applies to the overall plan.

      a. **Market Segmentation**: describe the market you are in, broken down by segments, i.e., commercial might include tilt-ups, tenant improvement, retail, etc.; also you should include a graph of how you are implementing your marketing and how successful you are at reaching your potential customers.

      b. **Market Analysis**: analyze the market and how you plan to achieve success.

      c. **Service Business Analysis**: describe in detail the Business Model and how it applies to the Business Plan.

            i. **Business Participants:** explain and define the businesses and organizations that will be potential partners and clients.

            ii. **Competition and Buying Patterns**: explain the competition, i.e. temp labor businesses, and how contractor and employers use these resources.

            iii. **Main Competitors:** list your competitors and give a brief analysis of their pros & cons.

5. **Strategy and Implementation Summary**: give a summary of your strategy to attract clients, and describe how you will implement your strategy.

    a. **Competitive Edge**: describe why you believe you have the competitive edge in the market.

    b. **Marketing Strategy**: in the sections which follow, describe in more detail your positioning statement, pricing, and promotion strategy.

        i. **Positioning Statement**: explain your position in the economics of the market and explain why you are viable in the market-place.

        ii. **Pricing Strategy**: explain your pricing and how it can be justified in the market-place. This is also where you would explain your crew mixes.

        iii. **Promotion Strategy:** describe how you will promote your business or organization.

    c. **Sales Strategy**: describe how the sales process works and how you will retain customers.

        i. **Sales Forecast**: describe how you plan to generate sales and also include a year by year graph of how you plan to obtain your sales goals.

        ii. **Milestones**: create a list of milestones, the dates associated with them and who is responsible for their execution. Also create a table and graph to associate these milestones.

6. **Management Summary**: describe in summary your management and style. Also explain who will be responsible for the daily operations.

    a. **Management Team**: list your proposed management team, and give a brief summary resume of their relevant experience and how that experience will help to implement your Business Plan.

b. **Management Team Gaps**: explain how you will handle management gaps in case the management team is unable to perform to the conditions you have set for them.

c. **Personnel Plan**: summarize your personnel expenditures for the years associated with the plan, with compensation increases from year to year; also include a table of the costs associated with the management personnel.

7. **Financial Plan**: should include the following summaries of financial information regarding the following projected items. Tables and graphs should accompany when appropriate.

a. **Important Assumptions**: the financial plan will depend on important assumptions, most of which should be shown in tables as annual assumptions. Some of the more important underlying assumptions will include:

- We assume a strong economy, without major recession.
- We assume the current services delivery method will not dramatically change.
- Interest rates, tax rates, and personnel burdens are based on conservative assumptions.

There should also be included in the important assumptions the **General Assumptions**, such as current interest rates, long term interest rates, etc.

b. **Key Financial Indicators**: a benchmark chart indicating your key financial indicators for at least the first three years or more. It should also foresee the growth from sales/organizing and a marginal reduction in operating expenses as the plan grows year by year.

c. **Break-even Analysis**: should include a table and chart summarizing your break-even analysis, with estimated monthly fixed costs of revenue targets per month that will cover your costs, when you expect to reach break-even, in regards to the business operating plan. The break-even should assume all variable costs at a percent of the revenue, also the revenue values as an aggregate measurement for all the types of services that will be offered.

d. **Projected Profit and Loss**: should be a standard accounting Profit and Loss Statement, which is inclusive of your projected assumptions year by year.

e. **Projected Cash Flow**: cash flow projections are critical to your success. The monthly cash flow should be shown in graph, with one bar representing the cash flow per month, and the other the monthly balance. The first few months are critical. It may be necessary to inject additional capital in this time frame if the need arises.

f. **Projected Balance Sheet**: the Balance Sheet should follow standard accounting practices and follow your projected assumptions.

g. **Business Ratios**: should be inclusive of the market-share assumptions and should be calculated in a few different mathematical formulas to show success or failure in your plan. This is where you will see what you need to adjust in order to stay on plan.

The Business Plan needs to be inclusive of all the issues discussed in this book. But first and foremost, it must be user-friendly to the clients (contractors/employers) that you will be selling your services to.

I believe that part of your Business Plan should adopt a co-op methodology in respect to the small contractors that are the majority of your potential market. Have solutions for their needs and concerns, and become a partner with them for both your success and their success. I am able to go into much more detail in my seminars on this subject.

The bottom-line: Construction unions must have a plan that will focus their attention on the present and future, and that makes them accountable for successes and failures. They owe this to their memberships, and their signatory contractors/employers, who are their business partners.

XIV. The Co-Op Methodology

Now that we have an effective business model, we will discuss some methods that will help improve the fragmented construction union industry.

As an industry, we have a tendency to eat our young. What I mean by that is that we make it too easy to obtain a contractor's license in most areas and by doing so, we set up the would-be contractor for failure. Since he thinks that because he has become efficient in his trade skills, he therefore knows how to be a contractor. The average start-up contracting company is in business for only 18 months, usually because of the lack of business and financial knowledge, along with the failure to plan.

There are distinct areas of expertise to this construction industry and the skill sets to be a successful craft-worker are not the same skill sets needed to be a contractor/businessman. I know of no state or province that requires you to have evidence that you know estimating, or have a certificate, or degree in construction estimating; or evidence that you understand accounting principles, or have a certificate or degree in accounting. The same holds true for the legal side of this business, as well.

The fact that our construction licensing authorities do not require prerequisites of evidence that the individual obtaining the license understands not only the skill sets of the trade, but also accounting, estimating, and construction law, helps to feed incompetence and unethical behavior in our industry. This in turn puts undo economic pressure on the competent and ethical contractors who play by the rules.

To make up for this breakdown in our industry, I believe we need to create, through our respective unions and associations, contractor co-ops much like farmers use. These co-ops would serve as a mentor or library which a small contractor could join to gain knowledge, share tools, and network in their trades and unite the small contractor majority in construction. Or in other words, de-fragment the industry. It would be a place where a would-be contractor could learn the risks and pitfalls to contracting before they make the leap into business.

XV. Cash is King

In any business venture, cash (also known as capital) is king. It is the amount of operating capital that keeps you in business. Now, just because your profit and loss statement says you're making a profit, this does not necessarily transfer to cash flow. In the construction business today, the average receivable is somewhere in the 80 to 90 days and over range. This means a contractor/employer has to have the appropriate operating capital to survive the 80 to 90 day cycle.

Look at the following Table #6, and let's analyze this table.

TABLE #6

	Jan	Feb	Mar	Apr	May
Project Expenses	($39,000)	($54,600)	($62,888)	($66,495)	($55,039)
Billings/Receivables	$45,000	$63,000	$72,563	$76,725	$63,506
Gross Profit	$6,000	$8,400	$9,675	$10,230	$8,467
Overhead Expenses	($4,800)	($5,938)	($7,514)	($5,938)	($5,938)
Net Profit, before taxes	$1,200	$2,462	$2,161	$4,292	$2,529
Actual Cash Received	$0	$0	$0	$40,500	$56,700
Contractors Investment	$43,800	$104,338	$174,740	$206,673	$210,950

Let's assume that we are a new business and we were able to secure a $400,000 project. The above referenced Table #6 is our actual financial breakdown as the months of the year transpire.

In January, the project's expenses were $39,000, and we were able to bill $45,000, making our gross profit $6,000. This would mean we had a 13.3% gross profit margin. That sounds like a pretty good return on investment. But we haven't calculated the business overhead yet.

What is business overhead? It is the cost of operating a business even when you have no projects to work on. It is what it costs to keep the doors open month to month whether or not you have any sales. So we see that for the month of January, our overhead cost was $4,800 just to keep the doors open for that particular month. That means that our net profit before taxes is $1,200 and that we had a 2.7% net profit margin. How good of a return on investment does that sound now?

We have shown a profit for the month of January of $1,200; but the critical issue in business is where the money is. Even though we billed $45,000 and show a profit of $1,200 on the books, this does not translate to actual dollars in the bank. In fact, we are now out of pocket $43,800 for the month of January. If we are using a credit line to operate our business, we now have to pay interest as well on the $43,800. Let's just assume we are using a bank line of credit to fund the business and it has an 8% annual interest rate. We have just added an additional $292 of overhead to our business for the next month by using the line of credit.

Look at the month of April in Table #6. You will see that we finally received some money that was due to us from our

January billing. But note that the customer/owner shorted us by $4,500. They have withheld a 10% retention from our billing so that the customer/owner has a hammer over our head; and it is a motivating factor for us, the contractor, to get the project finished so we can collect on that retention.

Let's look at April again in Table #6. By the end of that month, we are now $206,673 in the red; or in other words, we have invested $206,673 into the business. We have had to spend $206,673 in order to return $40,500, and it took us four months to do so. Sounds like a great business to be in! What do you think?

Let's look at the first quarter, which are the months of January, February, and March in Table #6. Now, for that quarter from an accounting perspective, you have $180,563 in sales, and you have spent $156,488 in cost of goods, which are the project expenses, giving you a gross profit of $24,075 for the first quarter. Your operating cost, or overhead, has cost you $18,252, which leaves you a net profit of $5,823 before taxes for the first quarter. Now remember you have not collected a dime yet, but Uncle Sam is looking for his taxes, and if you are operating as a proper business should, you will pay Uncle Sam his taxes based on this first quarter of estimated profit. Now bear in mind that you are, at this point in the cash flow side of the business, $174,740 in the red, not including the estimated quarterly taxes that you are going to have to pay as well.

As you can see the construction business is a cash intensive business; and on top of that, it is in a risky environment in regards to the installation. This makes it even more risky for an investor, if you are looking at the business on a return on investment-only mentality. The industry is not in a factory and does not have the controlled environment that a factory would have. It is a factory in the field, with lots of pitfalls that can befall the contractor/employer that may be beyond his control, making construction one of the most risky business ventures to be in, period.

Since you now know that the industry is cash intensive, and has a long cash flow cycle, you can see why cash is King in the construction business, and I haven't even dealt with the lien process.

Now you know why most construction businesses do not operate union. Simply put, cash does not flow in fast enough to compensate paying a crew of union men, at let's say, $45.00 per hour in costs in a composite crew environment, when you could pay $25.00 per hour in costs in a composite crew environment operating non-union.

Let's look at how much cash you would need to have a 15-man crew for 3 months at 40 hours per week operating union. You would need $351,000 in cash. Use that same crew operating non-union and you would need $195,000 in cash. That is a difference of $156,000. If you are a small business and just recently starting in business, you probably do not have the financial resources to operate in the union arena.

Why is it that the majority of contractors/employers usually stay about the same size? It's very simple, cash or operating capital along with risk assessment. The average contractor/employer finds a niche market in which he is able to be both competitive and profitable. He usually never strays too far from this niche because of the risks associated with expansion. So the construction union needs to have a business plan that understands the limitations and the risks associated with operating capital. You must also understand that some of your clientele and potential clientele are risk takers, while others are not, and this is usually due to the amount of capital they have at their discretion.

For construction unions to regain market share, they must be willing to recognize this cash flow truth and to construct a business plan that will take these issues into consideration. Keep in mind, construction unions: without these small construction firms, you will never control the marketplace. The industry is fragmented, so unite it.

XVI. Accounting for Success

Some of the concepts in this chapter came from Allen B. Bostrom, CPA, and he has a great book titled, "In the Black" -- a good read for any small business.

Fra Luca Pacioli, the father of modern accounting, said that three things were necessary for a successful business:

1. Adequate cash.
2. An adequate mathematician to work with the numbers.
3. A system that can show at a glance the financial position of the business or in other words, an accounting system.

Yet, the accounting function is the most neglected of the business functions. What I am now going to discuss is the accounting that is required to develop an accountability mindset to the construction unions.

It is hard when you are a non-profit organization to understand that you must profit to stay in business as an organization, but this is inclusive of for-profit and non-profit businesses and organizations. The purpose of this chapter is to show you the importance of a good accounting and business system and how the information derived from that system can be critical in improving the construction unions and the industry at large.

Accounting is the function of the business/organization that gathers data and information from all the different aspects of that business/organization. This information can then be used to develop knowledge and wisdom, and to make better business, organization, and industry decisions.

In a construction business, what is the most critical aspect of accounting? Job costing -- you must understand where your dollars are being spent. The project must have a budget, with line items that show expenditures that are budgeted from the estimate. Job costing accounting is the means by which you are able to recognize whether or not you are performing to the budget. It helps you to report and substantiate performance; it also helps you see patterns in efficiency or inefficiency, so you can better perform for your customer, the one who is buying your services.

What is the reason for any business or organization to be in existence? Profit. Profit may mean different things to different businesses or organizations; but without it, you will cease to exist.

For the for-profit business, profit means the ability to survive, grow, and diversify. For the non-profit business/organization, profit also means the ability to survive, grow, and diversify. The difference from a for-profit and non-profit business/organization is the reason for profit.

The for-profit business/organization reasons are to make money; have the ability to have more money in the bank at the end of the year than you had at the beginning of the year, and to give dividends to the share holders. The non-profit business/organization reasons are to usually provide a service to those it represents or associates with; but the non-profit's cash is completely dependent on the donations, dues, etc., it is able to receive.

The profitability of the non-profit is the ability to organize and influence people, organizations, etc., to accept what you represent, and therefore support your cause. But again, profit is the key and means to any business or organization and without profit you will eventually fade from existence.

We are now going to discuss the fundamental means to being in business. What are the three major functions of every business?

1. Marketing: the function of business that brings customers to you, and concludes in some sort of sale, contract, or arrangement.
2. Production: the function of business that deals with customers from the time of the first sale, contract, etc., through the entire relationship existence.
3. Accounting: the function of business that gathers data and information from all the different aspects of the business.

The goal of all business/organizations must be to become profitable. But to be profitable, you must be able to communicate the three major functions cohesively so that they become interrelated or create synergy. The more they become interrelated, the more profitable they will become, and synergy makes this possible.

The following Table #7 illustrates the three functions, marketing, production, and accounting, all operating independently with little regard for what is happening in the other two functions. The functions could be running well independently, but with little synergy. The center core, where all circles intersect, represents total profitability. You will see profitability is very small in Table #7.

Here are a few examples of why profitability is low:
- Marketing and sales are occurring, but no one tells production of new contracts that have just been signed, where contract language changes are involved.
- Production might be rolling along with no idea what labor costs are associated with the estimate, or if you are utilizing the appropriate crew mix or, if the wrong materials might be installed compared to what the estimate was.
- The project manager (accounting) seems to be tied to their desks, and never visit either the job site or a potential customer with the estimator.
- Within the separate functions, everything seems to be going well, except for the complaints about the other departments.

Table # 7

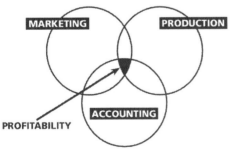

The above Table #7 shows the overlapping of the different circles indicating that little interaction is occurring among the different functions.

The above listed examples are typical of business or organizations. Communication and then accountability are the keys to success; good news and bad news need to be addressed in a rational way. This is how you are able to look at reality and address the approach you will take to rectify the mistakes and capitalize on the successes. Now, the business/organization that can interconnect these business functions, and that can create synergy within them, will be the ones that are the most profitable.

What the goal should be is depicted in Table #8.

Table # 8

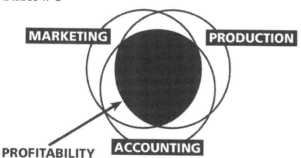

In the above Table #8, marketing works with production to make sure the right materials, labor, and crew mixes are ready at the right time. Accounting provides the critical information to both marketing and production to help in making profitable decisions. Thus, profitability is the means to better performance, and better performance means profitability; it is all interrelated.

The following ideology will help make for superior business/organization behaviors and principles as they are applied to the three major functions of business.

Marketing: Great customers do not just appear -- they are made!
- Nothing will happen until you make a sale!
- A deal is only good when it is good for both parties.
- Grow your business; if you are not growing, you are dying.

Production: Become the expert on what happens in the field of production in the business.
- Pour on the communication.
- Improve your internal procedures.
- Take what you have and make it better.
- Continually look to improve production methods.

Accounting: Stay accountable because profit is a necessity.
- Cash flow is King!
- Know your business well.
- Always plan for tomorrow.
- Take action on and eliminate waste.

If you are willing to use these steps to improve your union, business, or organization you will become more successful. Make your union accountable to the industry and to itself as well. Use these principles to gather data that is relevant to your market-share and be observant to the changes that are happening around you. In other words, take care of your customers.

Another factor which is killing the union construction industry is the return on investment (ROI) for the average contractor. The average union contractor has a rate of return of about 2 to 4 percent. With the rate of risk that the average project has, it makes it very difficult to attract contractor/employers to be union. It also keeps earnings-minded business investors out of the market. Unions must make a more profitable environment for the contractor/employer in order to attract fair-minded investors back into the construction industry.

Construction unions must also have a research and development mindset and continually evolve as the times and conditions change. Currently, unions are dinosaurs and reactionary in their approach to the changes in the economy; and typically, they react too little, too late.

Unions tend to focus on the dinosaur droppings to analyze problems. Instead of being ahead of the dinosaur to see what it eats and why, they wait to see what it ate that killed it. If the unions are to survive, they must be forward thinking, adaptable and accountable to continually changing conditions. Construction unions become accountable for your success!

XVII. What is Union Market-Share?

What is the market share of a local union? Very simple: it is how many contractors are signatory to your union agreement. These contractors reside in your local union's territory. An added bonus is the ability to have traveling contractors signatory to your local's agreement, those who do not reside in your geographical area.

Now most union leaders and members will argue that union market-share is determined by certain mathematical calculations and that is how you derive market-share. I will make the argument that using mathematical formulas are neither accurate nor appropriate in determining a union's market-share.

Let's look at what is considered union market-share by taking Riverside County, in the state of California in which I reside, as the example.

The US Census Bureau estimates for the year 2005 that there are 1,946,419 people residing in the County of Riverside. There is one widely accepted mathematical formula that says for every 500 people in a given society you will need one electrician, plumber, carpenter, etc. So if we are to use this formula in the County of Riverside, there should be 3,893 craft-workers working in each of their respective trades.

If the local union has an average membership of 600 members, then the projected union market-share would be about 15.4% of the available market using this formula. Now, what is the flaw in using this methodology? It makes very broad and inaccurate assumptions about your market-share. If you were to look at union membership records over the last ten to fifteen years, you would probably see that the membership in your respective local union areas have stayed about the same. Some memberships may have grown a little, but most have lost membership. It also does not take into account craft-workers who are on the out-of-work list, retirees, your local members who are working on the road in another area, signatory traveling contractors working craft-workers in your local union, etc.

Now, the US Census Bureau estimates for the year 1990 that there were 1,170,413 people residing in the County of Riverside, California. If your membership was 600 members in 1990, does that mean you had 25.6% of the available market? Let's just assume that in 1990, you had 500 members, meaning that the union market share would be 21% of the available market using the formula. The population of Riverside County, California has grown by 66.3% since 1990, and if we were to use the above assumptions in union membership, then the union grew by 20% since 1990. How have you, the union, faired in the marketplace since 1990? Not very well—you had 21% of the market in 1990; but now in 2005, you only have 15% of the market, and on top of that your union grew by 20%.

Now, I have not been able to get an accurate figure as to the number of signatory contractors during the above listed 15 year period. But there is one major trend that has occurred actually for about the last 30 years: the loss in signatory contractors and the inability to sign new contractors.

The critical success factor for union organizing, or business development, is the ability to sign employers to collective bargaining agreements. Unions will never be able to grow without doing this necessary function.

Let me make it very clear that a union without a signed employer is a social club. It is imperative for unions to have employers to be successful or even exist. Again I will reiterate, an employer does not need a union to exist. They have existed for millenniums without them, but unions need an employer to exist and it is the only way they can exist.

Now, to take the traditional bottom-up organizing tactics of recruiting craft-workers to join the union in an effort to monopolize the labor market in a fragmented construction market is neither realistic nor cost effective, if you are using only a bottom-up approach. Unions need employers to be viable; and if unions concentrated on signing employers, the craft-workers would naturally flow to them. What is more cost effective, tracking down 3,293 craft-workers to join your union and then getting them to all be in complete solidarity; or tracking down the employers in your local union, giving them a viable, realistic market condition and a collective bargaining agreement, and having their workforce come with them? It doesn't take a rocket scientist to see the logic focusing on signing the employer.

As I have discussed earlier in the book, it's time for construction unions to realize they are a human resource service business and they should take this approach to their organizing/business development methodology.

Now, what is the business of a construction union? It is simply a human resource service to its customer, the employer. Your business model should be to support employers in their need for craft-workers and craft-workers at every level that an employer, your customer, needs. I will ask the question again, now that you have come to terms that you, construction unions, are a human resource service business. This is how you should approach your business development, not by some mathematical formula that will never be truly accurate. It's very simple: if there are 50 contractors who operate businesses in your local union's area and you have 25 of them signatory to your collective bargaining agreement, you would have 50% of the available market, because your market is employers. Construction unions should not concern themselves with how much work an employer has. They should be concerned with how many of the employers residing in the local are signatory to the local union's collective bargaining agreement.

Let's assume that there are 200 contractors in your specific trade, representing the contractor base that resides in your geographical area. How many of those are signatory? I can guarantee you that there isn't enough. Now remember that only 20% of construction is done by 10 craft-workers and over firms, meaning that only 40 firms out of the possible 200 are probably in your union's current collective bargaining criteria. This leaves 160 contractors not in your current collective bargaining criteria. Now, the reality is that only about 30% of those 40 firms are signatory and possibly about 4% of the 160 small firms are signatory, proving that the current collective bargaining agreements do not meet the needs of the majority of the contractor base or to use business terms, the available market.

The collective bargaining agreements, which on a whole have been dwindling for the last 30 years, have dropped by 75% in just the last 15 years. This means that it is imperative to retool the collective bargaining agreement to meet the needs of your customer, the employer, who is primarily non-signatory with your local union. If your collective bargaining agreement cannot meet their needs or the needs of the smallest construction firm in your area, then it needs to be overhauled.

Any viable large business, which is what the construction unions are, will have a foothold on every type and sector of its market. It will invent a way to be in that market. Look at the auto industry and you will see that the large auto makers have models that meet the needs of every aspect of our economy— automobiles for the rich and the poor, the old and the young, etc. Construction unions must also be in every type, facet, and sector of our industry in order to thrive.

XVIII. Top Down vs. Bottom Up

To truly gain control of your market, you will need to have in place as part of your business plan, both a top-down and a bottom-up approach. What will sell one contractor may not sell another, so you cannot make assumptions that only one approach will work. You need both co-existing together to get maximum potential out of your efforts.

Your biggest bang for the buck will always be top-down organizing, simply because it takes signatory contractors in order to create market-share for a union and you also get instant additional membership for your union.

Bottom-up organizing is the most arduous and painstaking approach, but it is a necessary tool as well for your business plan. By salting an employer, it is the only way to evaluate how the potential new employer really operates. You can find out a lot of information for your potential sale of a collective bargaining agreement, which you would never truly know from a top-down approach. With bottom-up, you will find out things that would never be known in a top-down approach. You will get to know their field incentive philosophy, if they provide benefits, etc. In the top-down approaches, they may tell you they provide incentives, benefits, etc. but you will truly never know. You need someone on the ground willing to extract information.

Let me be very clear on this issue of top-down versus bottom-up organizing or business development. You must have both approaches in your business plan to be successful.

If you are only going to use one approach, then you will only reach at best 50% of your potential clients. Every contractor/employer has a different way of doing business; usually these are just subtle differences, or personality differences. What's going to work for one contractor/employer will not necessarily work for the next. Our collective bargaining agreements need to be inclusive of all types, shapes, and sizes of the contractor/employer base.

In any effective marketing campaign, you need to know the needs, wants, fears, concerns, limitations, advantages, disadvantages, and motivations that make up your clientele or potential clientele. In order to get accurate information, you need to know the above listed issues and the only effective way to do that is to have a top-down/bottom-up approach to your organizing/business development. Once again, what you may learn and translate in a top-down approach might be quite a different learning and translating experience from the bottom-up approach.

The main reason for taking both approaches is information in order to market, and police the industry. The sad fact of reality is that it will take the labor movement's efforts to police the industry since frankly, the ethical contractor/employer is usually too busy trying to keep his doors open to be on the front lines in the fight for policing the laws of this country, state, county, city, and etc.

Construction unions, you need to have in your business plan the budget and the personnel to police the laws that govern our industry to be able to persuade contractors and employers to help promote good ethics in this industry.

XIX. The Value of Risk

Why it is important to take risks to become successful? Everything in life revolves around risk and the individual or organization that learns how to wisely manage risk will usually find success in this life.

The forefathers and pioneers of the union movement knew they had to risk their lives, livelihoods, etc., in order to better their world and the world of their posterity. If it were not for these brave risk-taking men and women, we would never have been able to create the large middle class of this great country of ours. Now, because our unions no longer take risks, they have seen their memberships dwindle. In the mid- 1950s, the total workforce was about 50% union; today somewhere between 8% and 10% of the total workforce is union.

Unions of today remind me of the guy who believes he is falling off a cliff. He is hanging on to the last vine with both hands, thinking that somehow that vine is going to save his life. By not letting go with just one hand, to explore another alternative to his problem, he fails to come up with an alternative until after it is too late to be effective. Unions, you have dug yourselves into a large hole. Now you have to realize that it's time to take a risk and try a whole new concept in your history as a union in order to survive and pass this union onto your future brothers and sisters.

With risk there is sacrifice, having to do without, and realizing that what you were willing to sacrifice might never benefit you personally but it will benefit your posterity in the union movement. Sacrifice is what the founders of the union movement knew and truly understood—that you personally might never see the benefit of your sacrifice, but your hope and faith are that the next generation might benefit from your sacrifices. Because of the risk takers in the beginning of the labor movement, the construction unions eventually had 90% of the market in the 1950s and '60s.

Now, if the founders of the union movement could see what their unions had accomplished and then what they have lost, they would probably feel their sacrifices were in vain. Let's not let them down for their sacrifices to our industry.

Construction union leaders and members, it is now time to learn the value of risk taking, by creating a business plan of action, implementing it, and then adjusting it as necessary. Risk -- it is the only way to achieve success or to get your market back. Without risk, you will eventually disintegrate and die as an organization. In fact, you could possibly die even if you take the risk, but dying without taking a risk is stupidity.

Now, why do unions fail to take necessary risks? Fear! Fear of the unknown, fear that if I take a fork in the road I may get on the wrong side of that fork, fear of political reprisal, fear that I better not speak my mind because it may be unpopular. The reality for construction unions is that fear is killing them, and just as Franklin D. Roosevelt said almost 70 years ago, "The only thing we have to fear is fear itself." Fear is what is keeping the union movement from succeeding. The only way to fight fear is with risk taking. That is something that the founders of the union movement recognized; they asserted themselves and made something happen.

We, as a union movement, need to be grateful for risks and sacrifices made by the union forefathers and not let fear hold us down. North America is better off because of our union forefathers. Let's not sit idly by and not take a risk to better our future. Let's quit reacting to fear, and telling ourselves if we change the agreement to be more user-friendly then we will lose control. The fact is if you are not in the market, how can you control it?

XX. Conclusion and Summary

My hope is that as an industry, we will take a long hard look at ourselves, be honest, real and practical in our approach to better the industry we all make our living from.

We, as leaders in the construction industry, need to set aside our egos and analyze our conditions, not play petty politics and posturing. We then need to make practical decisions based on the realities of the fragmented state of our industry and to promote the industry in an ethical and healthy environment.

We, as an industry, need the labor movement to be well built and solid; but it also needs to be understanding to the pressures of the economy, and be willing to embrace change as it comes. Without unions, there is no check and balance to the employer, and that is not healthy for the economy as a whole. With less and less of a union voice on Capital Hill, it makes for less and less of a middle class.

Frankly, would you, the average union member, sign a collective bargaining agreement? If you cannot answer that question in less than thirty seconds, then your agreement is outdated and needs to come into line with the current world as we know it.

We should also encourage our current business managers to have a business degree and to require new ones to have a business degree. We should not be afraid to recruit business managers that are not affiliated with the trade: Managers that can look objectively at the business tasks that need to be accomplished, and who do not have a political agenda or motivation.

It's time for a new methodology that recognizes the truth that we are a fragmented industry. Create a business plan and model that reflects the realities of today, with the hopes for the future. But as you take the challenge to change, do not get caught up in what my good friend, Bob Segner, likes to say, "paralysis by analysis." Do not be afraid to take risks.

One last comment: the biggest weakness of change in the labor movement is the failure to follow through. I have been to countless seminars, motivational speeches, etc., all designed to get us motivated to positive action and change. But, what usually happens is that everyone is enthusiastic the hour after the seminar, speech, etc., but when the truth of having to follow through becomes reality, most of us prefer the sidelines. This means nothing gets done and we are still in the same spot we have been in, only now we have more knowledge, without any accountability.

The most important thing you will ever be able to do is to learn to follow through and then to learn to be accountable. This does not mean becoming a finger pointer, it means being responsible to your industry.

I hope construction union leaders will take this challenge to rise to the occasion, to improve the union movement in a fragmented industry, and to continually follow through and create success.

About the Author

Glenn G. De Soto is the Vice President of W.B. Walton Electric, Inc. Established in 1946, the company is located in Riverside, California, and is an IBEW/NECA contractor. He has over 25 years of experience in the electrical industry, from apprentice to contractor. He has salted non-union contractors during bottom-up organizing campaigns, testified before the National Labor Relations Board (NLRB), and won back-pay awards.

Currently, Glenn is on the Board of Directors of the Southern Sierra's Chapter of the National Electrical Contractors Association (NECA) and also a committee member of the IBEW/NECA Joint Apprenticeship and Training Committee of Riverside County, California. He is also a card carrying member of the International Brotherhood of Electrical Workers. He serves as a member of the NECA Manual of Labor Units Committee Task-force, and has served on various industry committees throughout his career. He has worked on various projects all over the United States, which has given him a broad viewpoint of the construction industry, which in turn has been a great educational tool for him.

Glenn has taught journeyman curriculum at the Riverside JATC, he has also taught the Foreman, Electrical Project Supervision, and Electrical Estimating courses sponsored by the Southern Sierra's Chapter of NECA. He has been a consultant to the industry in multiple facets from helping start-up companies, to helping companies with construction claims; he has also been a speaker at various industry meetings. He has a Bachelor's degree in Business Administration, and has completed multiple certificate, and continuing education courses.

Glenn resides in Southern California with his wife Cynthia, and children Clinton, September, Grace, and Joseph. He enjoys family vacations, and just being a family man. He also enjoys playing guitar and occasionally, as time permits, will perform with some of his friends.

Made in the USA
Lexington, KY
09 February 2012